UP CLOSE

REPTILES

PAUL HARRISON

W
FRANKLIN WATTS
LONDON·SYDNEY

Published in 2007 by Franklin Watts
Reprinted in 2008

Copyright © 2007 Arcturus Publishing Limited

Franklin Watts
338 Euston Road
London NW1 3BH

Franklin Watts Australia
Level 17/207 Kent Street
Sydney, NSW 2000

Author: Paul Harrison
Editor (new edition): Ella Fern
Designers (new edition): Steve West, Steve Flight

Picture credits: Nature Picture Library: 15 top; NHPA: front cover, title page, 2, 5 middle, bottom, 7 bottom, 8 top, bottom, 9, 10 middle, bottom, 12 top, bottom, 13 top, 14 top, bottom, 15 bottom, 17 middle left, 18, 19 top, bottom, 20 top, bottom, back cover; Oxford Scientific: 3, 4, 6, 7 top, 13 bottom, 15 middle, 16 top, bottom, 17 top, middle right, 21; Science Photo Library: 5 top, 11, 17 bottom; John White Photos: 10 top, 22.

A CIP catalogue record for this book is available from the British Library

Dewey number: 597.9

ISBN: 978-0-7496-7687-2

Printed in China

Franklin Watts is a division of Hachette Children's Books.

Contents

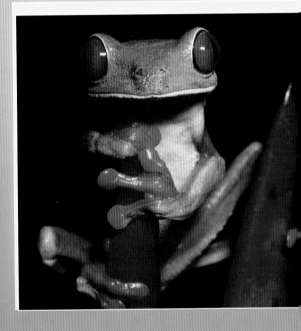

There are over seven thousand types of *reptile* and way more than four thousand kinds of *amphibian*. They come in lots of shapes and sizes, from giant lizards and huge tortoises to the tiniest of frogs.

ANCESTORS

Reptiles just aren't what they used to be. Even the biggest of today's lizards don't match up to their huge predecessors, the dinosaurs. That's right; those mighty monsters from the past were reptiles, too.

Reptile?

BIG AND SMALL

Anacondas, giant South American snakes, can grow up to 8–11 metres long. But some geckos don't grow longer than 2.5 centimetres.

People who study reptiles are called *herpetologists*.

SUN LOVERS

Reptiles live virtually anywhere where it's warm, but you won't find any on the cold ski slopes!

Body Bits

So, what makes a reptile what it is? All reptiles, big or small, have some things in common.

SLOW MORNINGS

Reptiles are cold-blooded, which means they can't generate their own body heat. Instead, they have to rely on the sun to warm them up. That's why they don't live in cold places.

LEGGY

All reptiles either have four legs or have ancestors which had four legs—including snakes. Of course, snakes lost their legs a long time ago.

Reptiles can shut their bodies down if they get too cold.

GOING UP

Reptiles are great climbers and this is due to their special clawed feet.

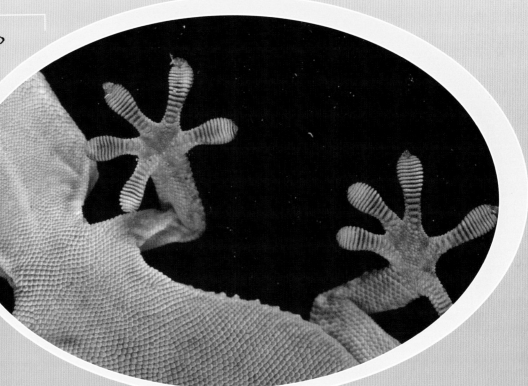

SCALES

All reptiles have scales, which are made from *keratin*—the same stuff your fingernails are made from. On some reptiles, such as crocodiles, the scales are joined together to form plates. This makes the skin tougher.

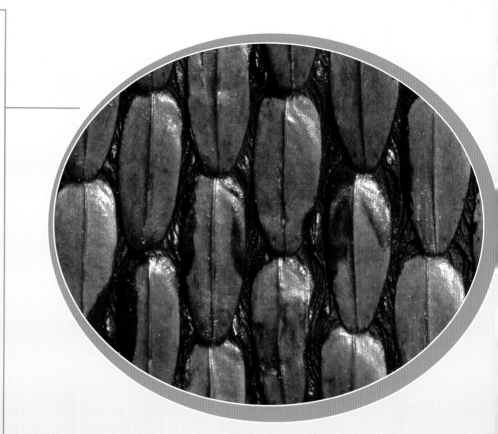

Here be Dragons

When explorers and traders went to foreign climates, they saw some of the biggest and most fearsome-looking reptiles. They came back with tales of dragons and gigantic beasts.

Komodo dragons have been known to eat children!

LIZARD KING

The heavyweights of the lizard world are the monitors, and king amongst them is the Komodo dragon.

PROUD PARENTS

Compared with many other reptiles, crocodiles are great parents! They make nests for their eggs and take care of their when they hatch.

SNAPPERS

There are over 20 species of *crocodilian*, including crocodiles, alligators, and caimans. The biggest are saltwater crocodiles which can grow to over 6 metres long.

SWIMMERS

Marine iguanas can stay underwater for up to an hour.

Snakes Alive

S nakes have a bad reputation, but in fact many snakes are harmless and run away from humans. Even the most poisonous ones will only bite if provoked or surprised.

FANG—TASTIC

Snakes' fangs are perfect for injecting poison into their prey.

Rattlesnakes have movable fangs which they can fold away when they're not needed.

VENOM

Some of the world's snakes are *venomous*, which means they inject poison into their prey when they bite them. The king cobra is so venomous that it can kill an elephant with a single bite.

BREAK OUT

Like other reptiles, most snakes lay eggs. Some snakes, like pythons, coil around their eggs to keep them warm until they hatch.

BIG SQUEEZE
The biggest snakes are the constrictors—snakes like pythons and boas. They crush their prey to death by wrapping them in their coils and squeezing really tightly.

GULP
Snakes have very flexible jaws but no teeth for chewing. They open their mouths as wide as possible and swallow their prey whole!

Hardly any snake bites are fatal.

13

Hard Shell

You might know them as slow-moving lettuce chompers, but some species travel thousands of kilometres across the oceans. Others can live longer than practically any other animal on earth.

HARD CASE

Turtles and tortoises all have shells to protect them. Some can bring their legs, head and tail into the shell for extra protection.

WHO'S WHO?

Tortoises live on land and turtles live in the water.

FLIPPING BRILLIANT

Sea turtles have large flippers instead of legs to help them swim. They only come on land to lay their eggs.

THREAT

Like many members of the reptile and amphibian families, turtles are under threat. Hunting and pollution are killing off some species.

GIANTS

Galapagos tortoises can measure over 1 metre from head to tail and they can live for up to 200 years!

15

Watery Wonders

A mphibians are different from reptiles, but just as amazing. They have much thinner skin than reptiles, and they lose moisture through their skin. This is why they always live near water.

DON'T TOUCH

When threatened, some amphibians ooze poison from their skin, which not only tastes bad but can kill some predators.

SURPRISE

Although most frogs live in damp places, you can even find them in the deserts of Australia. Desert frogs spend most of their time underground.

BRIGHT SPARK

Salamanders are secretive creatures that are often confused with lizards.

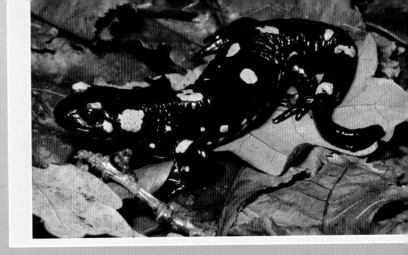

FROG OR TOAD?

If the skin is smooth it's a frog, if bumpy it's probably a toad.

SQUIRMY WORMY

This might look like a worm, but actually it's a *caecilian*. These blind, legless amphibians spend most of their lives underground.

Can you get warts from handling toads? Of course not!

Frills and Spills

R eptiles and amphibians
are capable of some
pretty amazing
behaviour.

WALKING ON WATER

The basilisk lizard can run over
water on two legs. This miraculous
behaviour earned it the name the
Jesus lizard.

TREE HOPPER

Some tree-dwelling lizards use special
flaps of skin to help them glide, like a
hang-glider, from tree to tree.

TAIL GAMES

This gecko has a large tail resembling a leaf. If a *predator* attacks the tail, the gecko allows it to simply drop off. It can then escape, and grow a new tail!

TRICKS

The chameleon has eyes which can move in opposite directions to each other and a long tongue which can shoot out to catch flies. It can even change colour to blend into its surroundings.

Some frogs have pouches like kangaroos.

CARING

The Suriname toad carries her eggs around on her back, where they sit embedded into her skin.

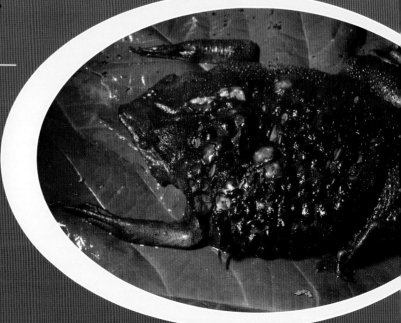

SHOWTIME

If it feels threatened, the frilled lizard of Australia puts on a show. It spreads out a frill around its head and makes a hissing noise. The frill makes the lizard look much bigger than it is and, hopefully, puts off the attacker.

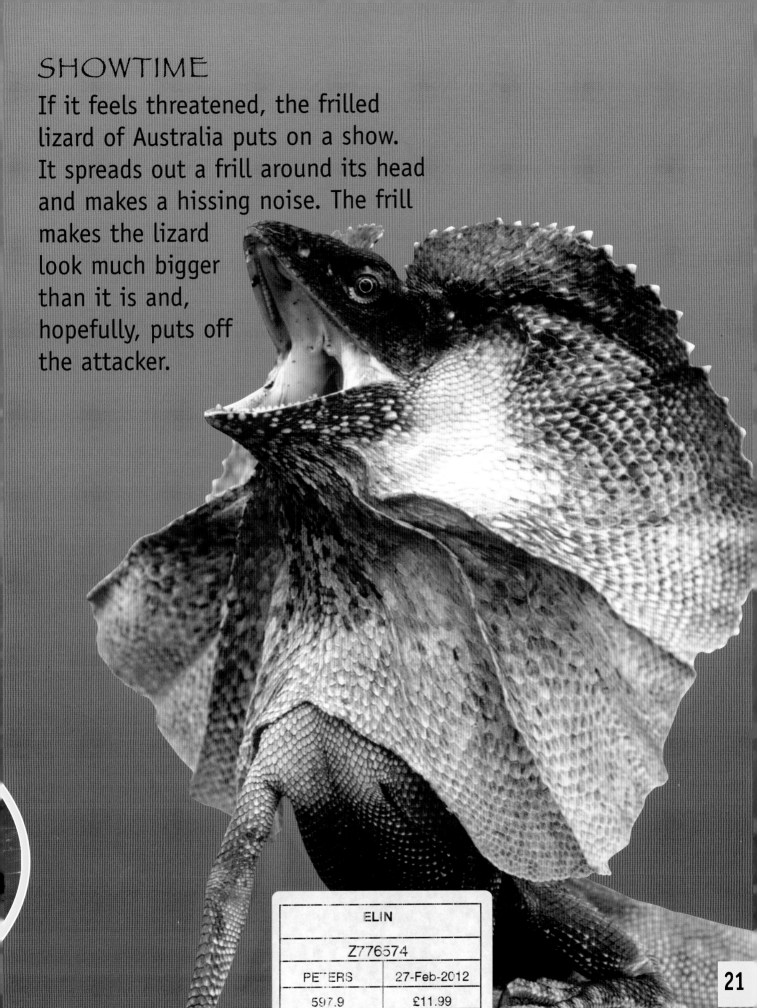

Glossary

Amphibian
A cold-blooded vertebrate (animal with a backbone) that can live on land and in water. Amphibians include frogs and salamanders.

Crocodilian
The family of reptiles that includes crocodiles, alligators and caimans.

Herpetologist
A person who studies reptiles.

Keratin
A type of hard protein that our hair and nails are made from.

Predator
An animal (a carnivore) that hunts and eats other animals.

Reptile
A cold-blooded vertebrate (animal with a backbone), covered in scales or a horny plate. Reptiles include lizards, snakes, crocodiles and turtles.

Venomous
A venomous creature is one that uses poison to attack its victims. The venom can be irritating, painful, or deadly.

Further Reading

Frog
Dorling Kindersley (Watch me Grow series), 2003

Illustrated Wildlife Encyclopedia
Barbara Taylor, Lorenz Books, 2004

I Wonder Why Snakes Shed Their Skin and Other Questions About Reptiles
Amanda O'Neill, Kingfisher, 1996

Reptiles
Mary Ling (editor), Dorling Kindersley (Eyewonder series), 2002

Reptiles
Colin McCarthy, Dorling Kindersley (Eyewitness series), 2000

Reptiles and Amphibians
John Farndon and Ann Kay, Miles Kelly Publishing, 2005

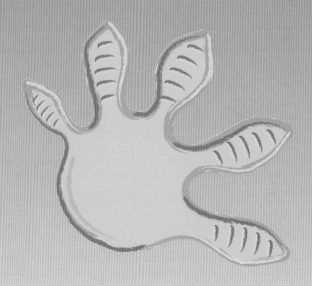

Index

TH 21/8/15